Spicy Salads

Recipes by Lee Geok Boi

PERIPLUS

Spicy Salads

Spicy Asian salads can be eaten as meals on their own but taste best when served with curries and simple boiled rice which brings out their sharp, often contrasting, flavours. Chillies are to Asian salads what fragrant oils, lemon juice and vinegars are to Western salads. Whether combined with shrimp paste to make Sambal Belacan or simply pounded with lime juice, chillies add that extra bite to a plate of fruit or greens. More flavour is then introduced with shallots, onion and garlic—occasionally fried but usually raw.

Spicy salads are not just tangy. They are often flavoured with fragrant herbs and spices such as coriander leaves, spring onions, basil, Chinese celery and ginger flower (*bunga kantan*). Herbs and roots such as galangal and lemongrass lift the simple cabbage and cucumber to great heights of gastronomic delight.

A delicious feature of spicy salads is the use of raw—often green—fruit. Green mangoes, belimbi (*belimbing asam*), ambarella (*buah kedondong*) and pineapple all pack a great tangy flavour. Green papaya, water apple (*jambu air*) and starfruit (*belimbing manis*) are chosen because of their texture or juiciness and the way they combine with the dressing or dip.

Vegetables may be raw or lightly blanched, or a salad might combine both raw and blanched vegetables. Because of the high protein content of Asian salads, when eaten with rice they make a complete meal. However, in the typical communal eating style of Southeast Asia, a fish or meat dish would often be present to accompany the salad and rice. Nevertheless, there are a few salads which make great meals in their own right. Dishes such as Gado-Gado, Thai Glass Noodle Salad and Suffed Beancurd may be taken alone or as part of a rice meal.

How to prepare light salads

From a dieter's point of view, many Asian salads have the added attraction of being relatively free of oil. The ingredients that give the salads their flavours—such as chillies, salt or fish sauce, lime juice, shallots and herbs—are essentially fat-free. For salads containing meat, use lean meat instead of belly pork. Both meat and seafood items are usually steamed or boiled.

The only exceptions to these fairly fat-free salads are those dishes calling for coconut milk or grated coconut, or which require an ingredient to be fried, such as Stuffed Beancurd. Beancurd could always be steamed or boiled instead of deep-fried though as the sauce would supply enough flavour to make the dish tasty for someone on a diet.

How to reduce preparation times

The preparation times for salads can be reduced by having some of the ingredients ready mixed. Sambal Belacan, which can be made ahead, bottled and refrigerated, keeps well. As do toasted and pounded peanuts, and toasted grated coconut. Nuoc mam, the combination of lime juice, fish sauce, chillies and garlic that is used in Vietnamese salads can also be prepared in advance.

Shallots, garlic and spring onions can be sliced or chopped and stored in boxes for several days although freshly prepared ingredients display more intense flavours. The bulk of the herbs and fragrant roots, however, can only be prepared just before mixing. Although commercial coconut milk is an easier option for many, do try to use fresh coconut milk wherever possible.

How to season salads

Because the flavours of spicy salads are sharp and distinctive, adjust them to suit personal preferences. Chillies can be very spicy or fairly bland. Tiny bird's-eye chillies are spicier than long, big chillies; and long, thin chillies are spicier than fat ones. Vary the amount of salt or fish sauce and type and amount of chillies to suit your taste.

How to shred green mango

To prepare shredded green, or young, mango, first peel the fruit and discard the skin. Take the peeled fruit in the palm of your hand and, with a chopping motion, make cuts lengthways over the mango. Cut down to the stone if possible.

The next step is to slice across the top of the mango (make sure to cut away from your body). This will yield long slender shreds of mango. Turn the mango in your hand and repeat both steps until you have shredded the whole fruit.

If you are not comfortable with this method, use a fine grater.

How to shred green papaya

To prepare shredded green, or young, papaya, first peel the fruit and discard the skin. Next, slice the papaya in half lengthways to expose the seeds. Scrape out the seeds and discard.

Shred the peeled papaya halves using a regular hand-held vegetable grater using the finest blade.

Sambal Belacan
(Fragrant Shrimp Paste Dip)

25 medium red chillies, deseeded
1 tablespoon shrimp paste (*belacan*), toasted

Pound the chillies with the toasted shrimp paste (*belacan*) until the chillies are fairly fine. Spoon the Sambal Belacan into a glass bottle and store in a refrigerator until needed.

Makes 250 ml (1 cup)
Preparation time: 10 mins

This Sambal Belacan is basic to many salads and can be made ahead and bottled. To make it more spicy, use some bird's-eye chillies.

Sambal Kacang (Spicy Peanut Dip)

1/2 tablespoon tamarind pulp soaked in 60 ml (1/4 cup) water
1/2 teaspoon ground dried red chillies
25 medium red chillies, deseeded
25 g onion (1/4 cup), peeled
1 teaspoon shrimp paste (*belacan*)
1 tablespoon lime juice
1 tablespoon sugar
Pinch of salt
75 g (1/2 cup) ground roasted peanuts

1. Stir and strain the tamarind and discard the solids.
2. Blend the tamarind water, chillies, onion and shrimp paste until fine.
3. Stir in the lime juice, sugar, salt and peanuts to make a thick dip.
4. Serve with vegetables such as cucumber, yam bean and cabbage, blanched vegetables or green fruit. Adjust the amount of lime juice to suit the acidity of the fruit or vegetable used.

Makes 250 ml (1 cup)
Preparation time: 10 mins

Hae Ko Dip (Prawn Paste Dip)

6 tablespoons black prawn paste
6 bird's-eye chillies, minced
2 tablespoon dark soy sauce
4 tablespoons sugar
3 tablespoons lime juice

Makes 250 ml (1 cup)
Preparation time: 10 mins

1. Combine all ingredients but omit the lime juice if using sour fruit.
2. Choose firm vegetables like cucumbers or yam beans. Sour or mild-flavoured fruits or fruits such as pineapple, green mango, belimbi (*belimbing asam*) or ambarella (*buah kedondong*) are suitable.

Nam Prik Dip (Fish Sauce Chilli Dip)

1 tablespoon dried shrimp
2 tablespoons oil
25 g (1/4 cup) shallots, coarsely chopped
6 bird's-eye chillies, minced
125 ml (1/2 cup) Thai fish sauce (*nam pla*)
100 g (1/2 cup) sugar
2 tablespoons lime juice

Makes 250 ml (1 cup)
Preparation time: 10 mins

1. Soften the dried shrimp in warm water, and remove any hard shell. Chop finely.
2. Heat the oil and sauté the shrimp until fragrant.
3. Add the shallots and chillies and continue to cook until the shallots are soft.
4. Add the fish sauce and sugar, stirring until the sugar is dissolved.
5. Cool, then pour into sterilised jar. Store in the refrigerator.
6. Use as a dip with any crisp, sour or mild-flavoured fruit such as green apple, green mango, water apple (*jambu air*) or belimbi (*belimbing asam*).

Omit, or reduce, the amount of lime juice in the recipe if using very sour fruits.

Palm Sugar Syrup

400 g (1 3/4 cups) palm sugar
250 ml (1 cup) water

Makes 425 ml (1 3/4 cups)
Preparation time: 20 mins

1. Melt the palm sugar in the water in a small saucepan.
2. Cool the syrup then sieve away the impurities and bottle the syrup. Store in the refrigerator.

Palm Sugar Syrup is not a dip in itself but is an important ingredient in several of the following salad recipes.

Thai Cuttlefish Salad

300 g (11 oz) cuttlefish
25 g (1/4 cup) thinly
  sliced shallots
2 bird's-eye chillies,
  minced
50 g (1/2 cup) thinly sliced
  onion
1 tablespoon finely
  shredded young ginger
2 1/2 tablespoons lime
  juice
1 1/2 tablespoons Thai
  fish sauce (*nam pla*)
50 g (1/2 cup) tomatoes,
  cut into wedges
1 spring onion, chopped
1 sprig chopped corian-
  der (cilantro) leaves

1/4 cup mint leaves,
  chopped
100 g (3 1/2 oz)
  coarsely shredded
  Chinese lettuce

Serves 4
Preparation time: 45 mins
Assembling time: 1 min

1. Clean the cuttlefish and cut into bite-sized pieces.
2. Blanch the cuttlefish in boiling water until it turns opaque. Remove immediately and drain, then place on a serving platter.
3. Combine the shallots, chillies, onion, ginger, lime juice and fish sauce.
4. Add the tomato wedges, spring onion, coriander and mint leaves.
5. Top with shredded lettuce and serve immediately with steamed rice.

Thai Raw Fish Salad

300 g (11 oz) salmon
  fillet
3 tablespoons juice of
  large green limes
2 tablespoons Thai fish
  sauce (*nam pla*)
2 bird's-eye chillies,
  minced
1 stalk lemongrass,
  smashed
150 g (3/4 cup) thinly
  sliced onion
2 kaffir lime leaves
100 g (3/4 cup) finely
  shredded Chinese
  lettuce
1 spring onion
  (scallion), chopped

2 sprigs (1/3 cup)
  coarsely chopped
  coriander (cilantro)
  leaves

Serves 4
Preparation time: 10 mins
Assembling time: 2 mins

1. Discard the skin and bones from the salmon and
   cut the fish into slices, about 1/2 x 4 cm
   (1/4 x 1 1/2 in).
2. Toss the fish in a mixture of lime juice, fish sauce,
   chillies, lemongrass, onion and lime leaves.
3. Add the remaining vegetables and toss well.
4. Remove the lemongrass and serve immediately.

*Fresh oysters may also be substituted for the
salmon.*

Yu Sheng
(Chinese New Year Raw Fish)

Salad

5 cm (2 in) young ginger, peeled and finely shredded
1 drop red food colouring
400 g (2 cups) peeled and finely shredded carrots
2 kaffir lime leaves, finely shredded
1 sprig (1/4 cup) coarsely chopped coriander leaves (cilantro)
10 g angelica (optional)
6 pickled leeks or onions, thinly sliced

Fish

2 tablespoons lime juice
1/2 teaspoon salt
1/4 teaspoon ground white pepper
1/4 teaspoon five spice powder
150 g (5 1/2 oz) fresh wolf herring or salmon, thinly sliced
150 g (1 cup) roasted peanuts, crushed
3 tablespoons toasted sesame seeds, crushed

Flour Crackers

50 g (1/2 cup) plain flour
1/4 teaspoon baking powder
1 1/2 tablespoons water
1 tablespoon beaten egg
1 tablespoon sugar
Pinch of salt

Dressing

3 tablespoons plum sauce
2 tablespoons oil
3 teaspoons sugar

Serves 4
Preparation time: 1 1/2 hours

Flour Crackers

1. Sift the flour, salt and baking powder into a medium bowl.
2. Combine the egg and water, and stir into the flour to form a soft dough. Roll out thinly onto a floured surface and cut into strips.
3. Heat the oil in a wok and deep-fry the strips of dough until crisp. Drain well, then crush coarsely and store in an air-tight jar.

The flour crackers can be prepared in advance or purchased from a Chinese confectionery shops.

Fish

1. In a small bowl, combine the lime juice, salt, pepper and five spice and pour over the fish, coating well. Sprinkle peanuts and sesame seeds over the top.

Salad

1. Colour the shredded ginger with the red food dye.
2. Arrange the carrots, ginger and other salad ingredients on a large serving platter.
3. Top with the seasoned fish anf flour crackers. Add the dressing.
4. All the diners mix the salad by lightly tossing the ingredients in the air together.

The eating of Yu Sheng during the Lunar New Year is a custom unique to Singapore but is spreading in the overseas Chinese world. The higher the toss, the better the luck will be for the diners.

Pineapple Kerabu

1/2 tablespoon Sambal
Belacan (see page 5)
1 1/2 tablespoons sugar
2 tablespoons dark soy
sauce
600 g (2 cups) coarsely
chopped ripe pineapple
1 shallot, thinly sliced

1. Combine the Sambal Belacan with the sugar and
soy sauce.
2. Stir in the pineapple and shallots and mix well.
3. Serve with steamed rice and other side dishes.

Serves 4
Preparation time: 15 mins

Green Mango Salad

1/2 tablespoon Sambal
Belacan (see page 5)
1 tablespoon black
shrimp paste
1 tablespoon sugar
2 tablespoons dark soy
sauce
650 g (2 cups) peeled
and shredded green
mango

1. Mix the Sambal Belacan with the black shrimp
paste, sugar and dark soy sauce.
2. Add the shredded mangoes and mix well.
3. Serve with steamed rice.

Serves 4
Preparation time: 15 mins

Thai Raw Vegetable Salad with Shrimp Paste Chilli Dip

800 g (1 lb 13 oz) raw
vegetables, choose any
combination:
Cabbage
Carrots
Cauliflower
Cucumber
Winged beans
Long beans
2 hard-boiled (hard
cooked) eggs, peeled
and halved

**Shrimp Paste
Chilli Dip**
1 coriander (cilantro) root
1/2 tablespoon shrimp
paste (*belacan*)
30 g (1/4 cup) dried
shrimps, soaked in water
6 bird's-eye chillies,
minced
3 cloves garlic
100 g (3 1/2 oz) poached,
peeled and coarsely
chopped small prawns
2 tablespoons lime juice
1/2 tablespoon fish sauce
1 tablespoon Palm Sugar
Syrup (see page 7)

1. Wash vegetables and peel if necessary. Cut into bite-sized pieces and soak for 5 minutes in cold water then drain well.
2. To prepare the Shrimp Paste Chilli Dip, pound the coriander root to obtain juice then set aside. Cook (broil) the shrimp paste under a grill or dry-fry until fragrant. Blend the toasted shrimp paste, drained dried shrimps, chillies and garlic. Transfer to a bowl, then stir in the coriander juice, chopped prawns, lime juice, fish sauce and Palm Sugar Syrup until well combined.
3. Serve the dip with the vegetables and eggs.

Serves 4
Preparation time: 20 mins   Assembling time: 2 mins

Singapore Rojak

100 g (4 cups) peeled and cubed cucumber
100 g (1/3 cup) peeled and cubed pineapple
100 g (1/2 cup) yam bean (jicama), cubed
50 g (2 oz) springy beancurd (*tempok*), cubed
100 g (3/4 cup) beansprouts
100 g (1/4 cup) water convolvulus (*kangkong*)
100 g (3 1/2 oz) jellyfish
100 g (3 1/2 oz) processed squid
1 tablespoon chopped ginger flower (*bunga kantan*) (optional)
1 deep-fried dough stick (*yu tiao*), sliced (optional)

Dressing
1 tablespoon tamarind pulp soaked in 2 tablespoons water
300 g (2 1/3 cups) roasted peanuts, crushed
6 tablespoons black shrimp paste
4 tablespoons sugar
3 tablespoons lime juice
1 tablespoon ground dried red chillies, fried in 1 teaspoon oil

1. Cut cucumber, pineapple, yam and beancurd intobite-sized pieces.
2. Blanch the beansprouts and water convolvulus for 10 seconds, remove and drain.
3. Clean the jellyfish and cut into strips; peel and clean the squid and cut into pieces.
4. To prepare the Dressing, stir and strain the tamarind water and discard any solids. Combine the tamarind water with two thirds of the crushed peanuts and all other Dressing ingredients in a salad bowl and mix well.
5. Add vegetables and other ingredients and mix well.
6. Garnish with remaining peanuts. Serve immediately.

The jellyfish and preserved squid for Singapore Rojak are readily available from Asian wet markets.

Serves 4
Preparation time: 30 mins Assembling time: 5 mins

Penang Fruit Rojak

800 g (1 lb 13 oz) fruit, choose any combination:
Ambarella (*buah kedondong*), see photo below
Green mango
Guava
Pineapple
Water apple (*jambu air*)
Starfruit
1 tablespoon chopped wild ginger flower (optional)

Dressing
1/2 tablespoon tamarind pulp soaked in 2 tablespoons water
3 tablespoons sugar
6 tablespoons black shrimp paste
1 tablespoon ground dried red chillies, fried in some oil
2 tablespoons lime juice
225 g (1 1/2 cups) ground toasted peanuts

1. Peel the fruit and cut into bite-sized pieces.
2. To prepare the tamarind water, stir and strain the tamarind and discard the solids.
3. Combine all the Dressing ingredients and garnish with the peanuts.
4. Stir the Dressing into the fruits in a large bowl.
5. Serve immediately.

Adjust the lime juice according to the sourness of the fruits.

Serves 4
Preparation time: 45 mins Assembling time: 5 mins

Urap
(Indonesian Coconut Salad)

50 g (1 cup) freshly
  grated coconut
1/2 tablespoon Sambal
  Belacan (see page 5)
10 g (1/3 oz) galangal,
  finely chopped
3 cloves garlic, finely
  chopped
2 tablespoons palm sugar
2 kaffir lime leaves, finely
  shredded
1/2 teaspoon salt
300 g (2 1/2 cups) long
  beans, cut into finger
  lengths and blanched
300 g (2 1/4 cups)
  beansprouts, blanched
2 tablespoons shallots,
  thinly sliced

1. Dry-fry the coconut in a frying pan over low heat
   for 4 to 5 minutes until the coconut turns golden
   brown.
2. Stir in the Sambal Belacan, galangal, garlic and
   palm sugar and continue to fry for a further
   3 minutes.
3. Remove from the heat and stir in the lime leaves
   and salt. Set aside to cool.
4. Mix the blanched vegetables and shallots with the
   cooled coconut mixture and serve at once with
   steamed rice.

Serves 4
Preparation time: 20 mins Assembling time: 5 mins

Pecel
(Indonesian Vegetable Salad)

100 g (1/4 cup) water convolvulus (*kangkong*)
50 g (1/4 cup) shredded cucumber
50 g (1/2 cup) thinly sliced long beans
50 g (1/3 cup) shredded cabbage
50 g (1/4 cup) shredded yam bean (jicama)
50 g (1/4 cup) shredded carrot
50 g (1/4 cup) cauli-flower, cut into small florets

Serves 4
Preparation time: 1 hour
Assembling time: 2 mins

Dressing:
2 tablespoons tamarind pulp soaked in 250 ml (1 cup) water
3 medium red chilies, seeded and chopped
1/2 tablespoon Sambal Belacan (see page 5)
1 teaspoon Palm Sugar Syrup (see page 7)
1 slice galangal
1 tablespoon chopped wild ginger flower (*bunga kantan*) (optional)
1/2 teaspoon salt
2 tablespoons fried shallots
1 tablespoon fried sliced garlic
225 g (1 cup) crushed roasted peanuts

1. Prepare the water convolvulus by removing the lower third of its stem. Remove any discoloured leaves and rinse well. Blanch for 5 seconds. Remove and immerse in ice cold water to stop the cooking process.
2. When cool, make bundles with one or two stalks, depending on the size and tie up the bundles with part of the stem.
3. Place the bundles and remaining vegetables in a deep serving dish.
4. To prepare the dressing, soak the tamarind in water then stir and strain, discarding the solids.
5. Blend the chillies and Sambal Belacan with the tamarind water until smooth.
6. Stir in the Palm Sugar Syrup, galangal, wild ginger flower, salt, shallots, garlic and peanuts.
7. Pour the dressing over the salad and serve.

Spicy Scallops Salad

300 g (11 oz) scallops
3 tablespoons juice of
  large green limes
2 bird's-eye chillies, thinly
  sliced
2 tablespoons Thai fish
  sauce (*nam pla*)
1 stalk lemongrass,
  smashed
100 g (1/2 cup) thinly
  sliced onion
150 g (1/2 cup) tomatoes,
  cut in wedges
1–2 sprigs (1/4 cup)
  coriander (cilantro)
  leaves
10 leaves Chinese
  lettuce, coarsely
  shredded

1. Blanch the scallops in boiling water for 2 minutes. Remove and drain well.
2. Place the scallops, lemongrass and onion in a serving dish.
3. Combine the lime juice, chillies and fish sauce and pour over the scallops.
4. Add the tomatoes, coriander leaves and lastly the shredded lettuce. Toss the salad lightly and serve zimmediately with steamed rice.

Serves 4
Preparation time: **15 mins** Assembling time: **2 mins**

Thai Mackerel Salad

200 g (7 oz) mackerel
1/2 teaspoon salt
4 tablespoons oil
2 tablespoons Thai fish
  sauce (*nam pla*)
3 tablespoons juice of
  large green limes
1 tablespoon sugar
25 g (1/2 cup) thinly
  sliced shallots
2 bird's-eye chillies, finely
  chopped
6 slices young ginger,
  finely shredded
2 kaffir lime leaves, finely
  shredded
35 g (1/3 cup) crushed
  roasted peanuts
1 sprig coriander
  (cilantro) leaves
400 g (14 1/2 oz)
  Chinese lettuce, torn
  into bite-sized pieces

1. Clean and scale the fish and marinate with salt for 10 minutes.
2. Heat the oil in a wok and fry the fish until nicely browned.
3. Cool then flake the flesh, discarding the skin and bones.
4. Combine the fish with all the other ingredients apart from the coriander and lettuce and toss well.
5. Arrange the lettuce in a serving dish and place the salad on top, then garnish with coriander leaves. Serve with rice.

Serves 4
Preparation time: 45 mins Assembling time: 5 mins

Vietnamese Papaya Salad

200 g (7 oz) small prawns
100 g (3 1/2 oz) belly
  pork
1 cup mint leaves,
  chopped
1/2 cup basil leaves, torn
  into strips
1 large green papaya,
  shredded (about 450 g,
  or 1 lb)

Dressing
2 tablespoons fish sauce
3 tablespoons juice of
  large green limes
4 cloves garlic, minced
4 bird's-eye chillies,
  minced

1. Steam or poach the prawns for 1 to 2 minutes until
   they turn pink. Cool, then peel.
2. Boil the pork in a little water for about 20 minutes
   or until cooked. Cool, then slice thinly.
3. Combine all the Dressing ingredients and stir well.
4. Toss the Dressing through the pork, prawns, mint
   and basil, and arrange this on top of the papaya.

Serves 4
Preparation time: 30 mins
Assembling time: 5 mins

Vietnamese Beansprout Salad

200 g (1 1/2 cups)
  beansprouts, tails
  removed
50 g (1/4 cup) finely
  shredded carrot
50 g (1/4 cup) thinly
  sliced onion
100 g (3 1/2 oz) belly
  pork, boiled and thinly
  sliced or 200 g (7 oz)
  small prawns, poached
  and peeled
2 tablespoons chopped
  mint leaves
2 tablespoons basil
  leaves, torn into strips
2 tablespoons toasted
  crushed peanuts

Dressing
2 tablespoons fish sauce
3 tablespoons juice of
  large green limes
4 cloves garlic, crushed
2 bird's-eye chillies,
  minced
1 tablespoon sugar
  (optional)

Serves 4
Preparation time: 2 hours
Assembling time: 10 mins

1. Combine all the Dressing ingredients and stir well.
2. Toss the Dressing through the beansprouts and set aside for at least 2 hours.
3. Add in the carrot, onion and belly pork (or prawns) and mix well.
4. Garnish with mint, basil and peanuts and serve with steamed rice.

Vietnamese Cucumber Salad

500 g (1 lb 2 oz)
  cucumber, quartered
  with soft centre
  removed
200 g (7 oz) small
  prawns, poached and
  peeled
1 cup mint leaves,
  chopped
1/2 cup basil leaves, torn
  into thin strips
1/2 teaspoon salt
1 spring onion (scallion),
  finely sliced diagonally

Dressing
2 tablespoons fish sauce
3 tablespoons juice from
  large green limes
4 tablespoons garlic
2 bird's-eye chillies
1 tablespoon sugar
  (optional)

1. Quarter the cucumber lengthways and remove the
   soft centre. Slice thinly, and place on a sheet of
   absorbent paper. Cover with another sheet of paper,
   and press down to remove any excess
   moisture.
2. To prepare the Dressing, mix all ingredients well.
3. Transfer the cucumber, prawns, mint, basil and salt
   to a serving dish. Toss the Dressing through the
   salad and garnish with spring onion.
4. Serve with steamed rice.

Serves 4
Preparation time: 20 mins Assembling time: 5 mins

Thai Mushroom Salad

500 g (1 lb 2 oz) oyster
  and/or straw mushrooms
200 g (7 oz) small prawns,
  steamed and shelled
25 g (1/4 cup) shallots,
  sliced thinly
1 spring onion (scallion),
  chopped
2 sprigs coriander (cilantro)
  leaves, chopped
Boiling water

Dressing
2 tablespoons fish sauce
3 tablespoons juice of
  large green limes
6 bird's-eye chillies, pounded
Juice of 2 pounded
  coriander roots

1. Wipe the mushrooms clean and cut in half or into bite-sized pieces if they are very large.
2. Blanch the mushrooms in a pot of boiling water for 5 to 10 seconds depending on the size of the pieces. Remove and drain well.
3. Place the prawns and mushrooms in a serving dish.
4. Rinse the coriander leaves and roots. Cut the roots off the stalks and pound (the roots) to a pulp.
5. Squeeze the juice onto the mushrooms and prawns. Stir in the lime juice, fish sauce, chillies and shallots and mix well.
6. Add the spring onions, coriander leaves and serve.

Serves 4
Preparation time: 25 mins Assembling time: 5 mins

Thai Papaya Salad

1 large green papaya
2 bird's-eye chillies, minced
3 tablespoons Thai fish sauce (*nam pla*)
3 tablespoons juice of large green limes
400 g (13 oz) small prawns, steamed or poached
150 g (1 1/2 cups) tomatoes, quartered and deseeded
1 spring onion (scallion), thinly sliced
1 sprig coriander (cilantro), roughly chopped
50 g (1/2 cup) thinly sliced shallots

1. Peel the papaya, quarter it lengthways and remove any seeds and soft centre.
2. Grate the papaya as thinly as possible, and place in a serving bowl.
3. Combine the chillies, fish sauce and lime juice and pour over the papaya.
4. Add the prawns, tomatoes, spring onion, coriander and shallots, and mix well.
5. Serve immediately with steamed rice.

Serves 4
Preparation time: 30 mins Assembling time: 5 mins

Karedog (Sundanese Vegetable Salad)

100 g (3/4 cup) cabbage, shredded

150 g (2/3 cup) cucumber, soft centre removed and shredded

30 g (1/4 cup) long beans, thinly sliced

50 g (1/2 cup) beansprouts, tails removed

2 tablespoons basil leaves, chopped

Dressing:

225 g (1 3/4 cups) roasted peanuts, crushed

4 bird's-eye chillies, minced

3 tablespoons lime juice

2 tablespoons Palm Sugar Syrup (see page 7)

1/2 teaspoon salt

Serves 4

Preparation time: 30 mins

Assembling time: 5 mins

1. To prepare the Dressing, mix all ingredients well.
2. Place the vegetables in a large serving bowl and pour the Dressing over the salad.

To ensure your salad is crisp, after washing dry vegetables on paper towel or spin in a salad spinner.

Grilled Aubergine

400 g (2 1/2 cups)
aubergine (eggplant)
30 g (1/4 cup) dried
shrimp, softened in
warm water
100 g (3 1/2 oz) small
prawns, poached and
peeled

Dressing
50 g (1/2 cup) shallots,
thinly sliced
3 tablespoons lime juice
1 teaspoon salt
1/2 tablespoon Sambal
Belacan (see page 5)

1. Wash aubergine, cut in half lengthways and grill or dry-roast until soft. For the long skinny variety it should take about 15 minutes. Cool then peel and cut into bite-sized pieces.
2. Rinse the dried shrimp, removing any hard bits, and pound or blend until smooth.
3. Combine all the Dressing ingredients then pour over the aubergine, shrimp and prawns.
4. Serve immediately with steamed rice.

Serves 4
Preparation time: 30 mins
Assembling time: 15 mins

Thai Green Mango Salad

500 g (2 cups) peeled and shredded green mango
2 tablespoons dried shrimps, soaked in water
25 g (1/4 cup) thinly sliced shallots
2 tablespoons oil
7 cloves garlic, thinly sliced
2 bird's-eye chillies, minced
200 g (7 oz) minced pork
2 tablespoons Thai fish sauce (*nam pla*)
1 teaspoon sugar
1/4 cup basil leaves, torn into thin strips
2 tablespoons toasted peanuts, crushed
1 sprig (1/4 cup) chopped coriander (cilantro) leaves

Serves 4
Preparation time: 30 mins
Assembling time: 10 mins

1. Remove any excess moisture from the mango with absorbent paper.
2. Remove any hard shells from shrimps then drain and chop them coarsely.
3. Sauté the shallots in oil until lightly golden then remove from the oil and set aside.
4. Quickly cook the garlic, taking care not to burn it. Remove from the oil and set aside.
5. Add the dried shrimp and chillies to the pan and sauté until fragrant. Drain off any excess oil.
6. Stir in the minced pork, then the fish sauce and sugar. Remove from the heat and cool.
7. Tear the basil leaves into thin strips and combine with the pork, fried garlic and shallots, mango, peanuts and coriander leaves, then pile the salad onto a serving platter. Serve with steamed rice.

Cabbage, Wood Ears and Chicken Kerabu

15 g (1/4 cup) wood ear
mushrooms, softened in
warm water
50 g (1/2 cup) thinly
sliced shallots
1 tablespoon wild ginger
flower (*bunga kantan*)
1 tablespoon Sambal
Belacan (see page 5)
3 tablespoons lime juice
1 teaspoon salt
200 g (7 oz) chicken,
poached and shredded
200 g (1 1/2 cups) finely
shredded cabbage
1 spring onion (scallion),
chopped

1. Clean softened wood ears by trimming off any woody or sandy bits. If mushrooms are large, cut them into small strips.
2. Cook the wood ears in boiling water for about 5 to 10 minutes depending on their thickness.
3. Mix the sliced shallots, ginger flower, Sambal Belacan, lime juice, salt and wood ears together.
4. Add the chicken, cabbage and spring onion and mix well.
5. Serve immediately with steamed rice.

Serves 4
Preparation time: 30 mins Assembling time: 2 mins

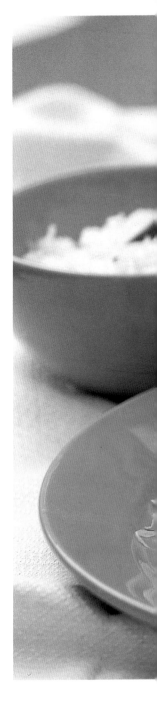

Chicken Kerabu

300 g (11 oz) chicken,
  steamed
450 g (1 lb) cabbage,
  cut into 2 cm (3/4 in)
  squares
25 g (1/4 cup) thinly
  sliced shallots
2 tablespoons lime juice
1 tablespoon Sambal
  Belacan (see page 5)
1 teaspoon salt
75 ml (1/4 cup) Fresh
  Coconut Cream

1. Cut the steamed chicken into 1 cm (1/2 in) cubes.
2. Blanch the cabbage by placing it in a sieve and
   pouring hot water over it. The cabbage should
   remain crisp. Drain well.
3. Combine the shallots, Sambal Belacan, lime juice
   and salt together then add the chicken and cabbage.
   Stir in the thick coconut milk and serve with
   steamed rice.

Fresh Coconut Cream

75 g (1 1/2 cups) freshly
  grated coconut, tightly
  packed
75 ml (1/4 cup) water

1. To prepare Fresh Coconut Cream, mix grated
   coconut with water in a cheese cloth and strain.

Serves 4
Preparation time: 30 mins Assembling time: 15 mins

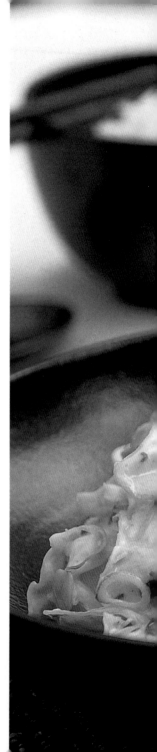

Sambal Timun
(Pork & Cucumber Salad)

200 g (7 oz) pork belly
250 g (1 cup) cucumber
2 tablespoons dried
   shrimp, soaked, cleaned
   and pounded until
   smooth

Dressing:
25 g (1/4 cup) shallots,
   thinly sliced
1/2 tablespoon Sambal
   Belacan (see page 5)
2 tablespoons lime juice
1/2 teaspoon salt

1. Simmer the pork belly in water for about 20 minutes until it is cooked through. Cool, then slice thinly.
2. Peel the cucumber and quarter it lengthways. Remove the soft centre and slice into bite-size-pieces.
3. To prepare the Dressing, mix all the ingredients thoroughly.
4. Combine the Dressing with the dried shrimp, pork and cucumber.
5. Serve with steamed rice.

Serves 4
Preparation time: 30 mins Assembling time: 15 mins

Starfruit and Pork Salad

150 g (5 1/2 oz) pork
  belly, grilled or boiled
1 tablespoon dried
  shrimps, soaked in
  water
300 g (3 cups) starfruit
1/2 teaspoon salt
1 tablespoon Sambal
  Belacan (see page 5)
25 g (1/4 cup) shallots,
  thinly sliced
1 spring onion (scallion),
  chopped

Serves 4
Preparation time: **20 mins**
Assembling time: **5 mins**

1. Slice pork into thin strips and set aside.
2. Drain shrimps and remove any hard shell. Pound
   until smooth.
3. Rinse the starfruit and trim the edges. Slice thinly.
4. Combine the shrimps with the salt, Sambal Belacan
   and shallots and toss with the sliced starfruit and
   sliced pork. Garnish with spring onion.

*Belimbi (belimbing asam) is a variety of round green
starfruit, or carambola, with a marked sour flavour
and makes a good substitute for the sweeter
starfruit (belimbing manis).*

Nasi Ulam (Rice Salad)

100 g (3 1/2 oz) salted threadfin fish (*ikan kurau*)
2 tablespoons oil
100 g (3/4 cup) shredded cabbage
1 tablespoon Sambal Belacan (see page 5)
25 g (1/4 cup) thinly sliced shallots
1 tablespoon lime juice
1 kg (6 cups) hot cooked rice
1 teaspoon salt
200 g (2/3 cup) peeled and shredded cucumber
5 sprigs (1 cup) coriander (cilantro) leaves
1/2 cup fresh basil leaves

1. Rinse the salted fish and dry with kitchen towel. Slice thinly.
2. Heat the oil in a pan and fry the salted fish until fragrant and crisp. Remove the fish from pan and cool.
3. Pound the fish until smooth then set aside.
4. Blanch the cabbage by placing it in a sieve and pouring boiling water over it. Drain and dry, removing as much excess water as possible.
5. Combine the Sambal Belacan with the shallots and lime juice.
6. Toss with the rice, salt, cabbage and salted fish until thoroughly mixed.
7. Add the cucumber, coriander and basil leaves and serve immediately.

Serves 4
Preparation time: 30 mins Assembling time: 15 mins

Gado-Gado
(Indonesian Mixed Salad)

400 g (2 cups) potatoes, peeled and cubed

120 g (1 cup) bean-sprouts

120 g (1 cup) coarsely shredded Chinese cabbage

120 g (1 cup) long beans

3 tablespoons oil

50 g (1 3/4 oz) soya bean cake (*tempeh*)

300 g (1 cup) firm bean-curd

120 g (1/2 cup) cucumber, sliced into finger lengths

5 leaves Chinese lettuce, washed and dried

2 hard-boiled eggs, peeled and halved

12 fried prawn crackers (*kerupuk*, or *kerupuk emping*)

Dressing

3 tablespoons ground dried red chillies

100 g (1 cup) shallots

7 cloves garlic

1 teaspoon shrimp paste (*belacan*)

2 tablespoons water

2 tablespoons oil

500 ml (2 cups) water

2 tablespoons rice vinegar

1 1/4 teaspoons salt

5 tablespoons sugar

300 g (2 cups) roasted peanuts, crushed

1. Boil the potatoes until firm and tender, then drain and divide between four serving bowls.

2. Blanch the beansprouts for 10 seconds, remove and plunge them briefly into ice cold water. Repeat for the cabbage. Drain both well and divide between each bowl.

3. Cut long beans to finger lengths then boil until tender and place in each bowl.

4. Heat the oil in a pan or wok and fry the tempeh on both sides until brown. Remove and drain on kitchen towel, cube then place in each bowl.

5. Pat the beancurd dry with paper towel and fry in the oil until brown on both sides. Remove and cut into cubes and divide between the four bowls.

6. Divide the remaining vegetables into each bowl and top with half an egg.

7. Prepare the Dressing and pour over the vegetables. Garnish with *kerupuk*.

Dressing

1. Blend the dried chillies, shallots, garlic and shrimp paste with 2 tablespoons water until smooth.

2. Heat the oil and sauté the blended ingredients until fragrant.

3. Add the water, vinegar, salt, sugar and peanuts and bring to the boil. Reduce the heat and simmer for another 10 minutes.

Serves 4

Preparation time: 1 hour Assembling time: 30 mins

Prawn Kerabu

250 g (1 cup) shredded
  cabbage
25 g (1/4 cup) thinly
  sliced shallots
2 tablespoons Sambal
  Belacan (see page 5)
1 tablespoon chopped
  wild ginger flower
  (*bunga kantan*)
  (optional)
3 tablespoons lime juice
1 teaspoon salt
300 g (11 oz) large prawns,
  poached and peeled
280 g (1 cup) shredded
  cucumber
250 ml (1 cup) thick
  coconut milk

1. Briefly blanch the shredded cabbage by pouring
   boiling water over it, then drain.
2. Combine the shallots, Sambal Belacan, wild ginger
   flower, lime juice and salt, then add the prawns,
   cucumber, cabbage and coconut milk. Mix well.
3. Serve immediately with steamed rice.

Serves 4
Preparation time: 30 mins   Assembling time: 10 mins

Kerabu Bee Hoon (Rice Noodle Salad)

30 g (1/4 cup) dried shrimps, soaked in water for 10 minutes

200 g (7 oz) dry rice vermicelli noodles (*mifen*)

1 1/2 tablespoons Sambal Belacan (see page 5)

50 g (1/2 cup) finely sliced shallots

50 g (1 cup) finely grated coconut, toasted

3 tablespoons lime juice

1 teaspoon salt

200 g (1 1/2 cups) beansprouts, blanched

100 g (1 cup) chopped spring onions (scallions), coriander (cilantro) leaves and Chinese parsley

1. Remove any hard bits from shrimps, drain and blend until smooth.
2. Cook dry noodles in boiling water for about 3-5 minutes until noodles are almost done. Drain.
3. Combine Sambal Belacan, shallots, dried shrimp, grated coconut, lime juice and salt.
4. Add the beansprouts, then mix in the rice noodles and chopped herbs.
5. Serve immediately.

Serves 4
Preparation time: 30 mins Assembling time: 15 mins

Thai Glass Noodles Salad

100 g (3 1/2 oz) small squid, cleaned and cut into rings

200 g (7 oz) small or medium prawns, poached and peeled

1 tablespoon chopped wood ear mushrooms, soaked in warm water and drained

75 g (3 oz) glass noodles

3 sprigs coriander (cilantro) with roots

4 bird's-eye chillies, deseeded and finely sliced

2 1/2 tablespoons juice of large green limes

2 1/2 tablespoons Thai fish sauce (*nam pla*)

1 large spring onion (scallion), chopped

50 g (1/2 cup) shallots, thinly sliced

Serves 4
Preparation time: 20 mins
Assembling time: 20 mins

1. Steam or poach squid for 1 minute in a little boiling water until tender (do not overcook). Drain and set aside.

2. Steam or poach prawns for 3 minutes or until pink. Drain and leave to cool.

3. Remove the heads and shells from the prawns, leaving the tails intact. Insert a knife along the centre of the backs and remove intestinal tracts.

4. Blanch the mushrooms in boiling water for 2 minutes, drain and set aside.

5. Cook glass noodles in boiling water for 10 minutes or until soft. Drain and keep the noodles warm.

6. Wash the coriander plants well. Remove the leaves and set aside. Remove the roots 1 cm (1/2 in) above the joint and discard the stems. Pound the roots to extract the juice and pour over the noodles. Mix well.

7. Stir in the minced chillies, lime juice .and fish sauce.

8. Mix through the remaining ingredients. Serve at once with steamed rice.

Joo Hoo Char
(Yam Bean in Lettuce Leaf Packets)

50 g (1 3/4 oz) dried
  squid
2 tablespoons oil
3 cloves garlic, chopped
600 g (1 lb 6 oz) peeled
  and finely shredded yam
  bean (jicama)
1 1/2 tablespoons light
  soy sauce
2 drops dark soy sauce
375 ml (1 1/2 cups)
  prawn, chicken or pork
  stock
1/4 teaspoon salt
20 Chinese lettuce leaves

1. Clean the squid in salted water. Remove the central plastic-like cartilage and soak in 1 tablespoon water until soft. Drain, reserving the water, then finely slice the squid.
2. Heat the oil in a wok and sauté the garlic for 5 seconds then add the squid and its water, the yam bean, light soy sauce, stock and salt. Bring to the boil.
3. Add a few drops of dark soy sauce to colour the yam mixture.
4. Simmer gently for 15 minutes or until the yam bean is tender.
5. To serve, spoon some of the vegetable and squid mixture onto a lettuce leaf and roll it up into a packet.

Serves 4
Preparation time: 30 mins Assembling time: 15 mins

Vietnamese Chicken Salad

450 g (1 lb) cabbage
200 g (7 oz) chicken breast, poached and shredded
25 g (1/4 cup) thinly sliced shallots
3 sprigs (1/2 cup) coriander (cilantro) leaves
1 large spring onion, finely sliced

Dressing
2 tablespoons fish sauce
3 tablespoons juice of large green limes
4 cloves garlic, crushed
2 bird's-eye chillies, finely minced

Garnish
3 tablespoons toasted, chopped peanuts
1 tablespoon fried shallots

1. Remove the central stem from the cabbage, and shred finely.
2. Combine the cabbage, chicken, shallots, coriander and spring onion in a large serving bowl.
3. Combine all the Dressing ingredients and stir well.
4. Add the Dressing to salad and toss thoroughly.
5. Garnish with peanuts and fried shallots and serve with steamed rice.

Serves 4
Preparation time: 30 mins Assembling time: 5 mins

Thai Beef Salad

1 large red onion, peeled
  and cut into thin rings
500 g (1 lb 2 oz) beef
  tenderloin, roasted or
  grilled, sliced thinly
200 g (2/3 cup) Chinese
  lettuce, leaves separated
  and rinsed well
4 spring onions (scallions),
  chopped
200 g (3/4 cup)
  cucumber, sliced
100 g (1/3 cup) toma-
  toes, cut into small
  wedges, or sliced
2 sprigs (1/4 cup) coriander (cilantro) leaves
1 sprig mint leaves

Dressing
2 cloves garlic, peeled
5 fresh red chillies, seeds
  removed
1 bunch coriander leaves,
  rinsed clean and
  chopped finely
1 tablespoon sugar
2 teaspoons Thai fish
  sauce (*nam pla*)
1 tablespoon fresh lime
  juice
1/2 teaspoon salt
1/2 teaspoon freshly
  grated black pepper

1. Prepare the Dressing by pounding the garlic, chillies, coriander leaves and sugar to a fine paste.
   Transfer the paste to a small bowl and stir in the
   fish sauce, lime juice, sugar, salt and black pepper.
2. Stir in the onion rings and sliced beef and set aside
   for about 15 minutes.
3. Arrange the lettuce leaves on a large serving dish
   and spread the dressed meat on top of the leaves.
4. Arrange the spring onions, cucumber slices and
   tomato wedges on the lettuce leaves.
5. Spread the coriander and mint leaves over the salad.

*An alternative way of preparing the meat is way is
to cook sliced raw beef with the Dressing paste.
Heat 1 tablespoon oil in a wok, and sauté the
pounded paste for several minutes before adding
the beef. Sauté for 30 to 60 seconds more, depending on how well done you like your beef. Stir in the
fish sauce, lime juice, salt and grated black pepper
when beef is done.*

Serves 4
Preparation time: **30 mins** Assembling time: **5 mins**

Stuffed Beancurd

100 g (3/4 cup)
  blanched beansprouts
100 g (1/3 cup) shred-
  ded cucumber
8 small firm beancurd
  cakes (about 100 g or 3
  1/2 oz each)
6 tablespoons oil

Dressing:

5 fresh red chillies
3 slices ginger
1 clove garlic, chopped
1 tablespoon rice vinegar
125 ml (1/2 cup) water
1 teaspoon sugar
1/2 teaspoon salt
1 sprig chopped corian-
  der (cilantro) leaves

1. To prepare the Dressing, combine all the ingredients apart from the coriander leaves in a bowl, stir
   well then sprinkle coriander leaves on top.
2. Mix the beansprouts and cucumber and set aside.
3. Make a slit along one side of the beancurd, scoop-
   ing some out to form a pocket. Taking care not to
   tear the sides, stuff with the vegetable mixture.
4. In a wok or frying pan, brown the beancurd quickly
   in hot oil. To prevent it sticking, only turn the beancurd when it is brown. Drain on a wire rack.
5. Place beancurd on individual serving plates and
   cover with the dressing. Serve with or without rice.

Serves 4
Preparation time: 30 mins Assembling time: 15 mins

Tauhu Goreng (Fried Beancurd)

6 tablespoons oil
4 firm beancurd cakes,
  (total about 800 g)
400 g (3 cup) beansprouts,
  blanched
200 g (3/4 cup)
  cucumber, sliced

Dressing
1 tablespoon tamarind
  pulp soaked in 250 ml
  (1 cup) water
1 cup (150 g) toasted and
  blended peanuts
6 cloves garlic, pounded
1 tablespoon Sambal
  Belacan (see page 5)
1/2 tablespoon lime juice
100 g (1/2 cup) sugar
2 tablespoons dark soy sauce

1. To prepare the Dressing, strain the tamarind juice and discard the seeds. Then put all the ingredients into a small saucepan and bring to the boil. Simmer for 5 minutes.
2. Heat the oil in a frying pan and fry a beancurd cake. When the beancurd is brown, turn and fry the other side. Repeat with all four pieces.
3. Divide the beancurd, beansprouts and cucumber into four serving plates.
4. Pour the Dressing over the beancurd and vegetables.

Serves 4
Preparation time: 30 mins   Assembling time: 5 mins

Taupok Pau
(Stuffed Spongy Beancurd)

330 g (2 1/2 cups)
beansprouts, blanched
180 g (2/3 cup) shred-
ded cucumber
150 g (5 1/2 oz) spongy
beancurd (*taupok*), slit
open on one side

Dressing
1 tablespoon tamarind
pulp soaked in 60 ml
(1/4 cup) water
3 tablespoons lime juice
1/2 teaspoon Sambal
Belacan (see page 5)
2 tablespoons sugar
4 tablespoons black
shrimp paste (*hae ko*)
150 g (1 cup) roasted
peanuts, crushed

1. Blanch the beansprouts in boiling water for 5
   seconds, drain well and cool. Combine the
   beansprouts with the shredded cucumber and
   mix well.
2. Stuff the beancurd with the vegetable mixture.
3. Grill (broil) the beancurd for 5 minutes on each
   side, leaving it crisp but not singed.
4. Cut each beancurd into four pieces and transfer to
   a serving plate.
5. To prepare the Dressing, stir and strain the
   tamarind and remove any solids. Mix tamarind
   water with all other ingredients and stir until thick.
6. Spoon the Dressing over the beancurd and serve
   immediately with rice.

Serves 4
Preparation time: 30 mins Assembling time: 15 mins

Index

Sambal Belacan, 5
Cabbage, Wood Ears and
  Chicken Kerabu, 38
Chicken Kerabu, 40
Chinese New Year Raw
  Fish, 10
Fish Sauce Chilli Dip, 7
Fragrant Shrimp Paste
  Dip, 5
Fried Beancurd, 63

Cold Salads
  Green Mango Salad, 12
  Pecel, 22
  Penang Fruit Rojak, 18
  Pineapple Kerabu, 12
  Singapore Rojak, 16
  Thai Cucumber
    Salad, 10
  Thai Cuttlefish Salad, 8
  Thai Raw Fish Salad, 9
  Thai Raw Vegetable Salad
    with Shrimp Paste
    Chilli Dip, 14
  Urap, 21
  Yu Sheng, 10

Dips
  Hae Ko Dip, 6
  Nam Prik Dip, 7
  Nam Prik Kapi Dip (Fish
    Sauce Prawn Paste
    Chilli Dip), 14
  Sambal Belacan, 5
  Sambal Kacang, 5
Gado-Gado, 48
Green Mango Salad, 12
Grilled Aubergine, 35
Hae Ko Dip, 6
Indonesian Coconut
  Salad, 21
Indonesian Vegetable
  Salad, 22
Joo Hoo Char, 54
Karedog, 34
Kerabu Bee Hoon, 51
Kerabu Chicken, 30
Mango, 4
Nam Prik Dip, 7

Nam Prik Kapi Dip
  (Fish Sauce Prawn Paste
  Chilli Dip), 14
Nasi Ulam, 47
Palm Sugar Syrup, 7
Papaya, 4
Pecel, 22
Penang Fruit Rojak, 18
Pineapple Kerabu, 12
Pork & Cucumber Salad, 42
Prawn Kerabu, 50
Prawn Paste Dip, 6
Rice Noodle Salad, 51
Rice Salad, 47

Salad Meals
  Gado-Gado, 48
  Joo Hoo Char, 54
  Kerabu Bee Hoon, 51
  Nasi Ulam, 47
  Prawn Kerabu, 50
  Stuffed Beancurd, 60
  Tauhu Goreng, 63
  Taupok Pau, 62
  Thai Beef Salad, 59
  Thai Glass Noodles
    Salad, 52
  Vietnamese Chicken
    Salad, 56
Sambal Kacang, 16
Sambal Timun, 42
Singapore Rojak, 16
Spicy Scallops Salad, 24
Squid in Lettuce Leaf
  Packets, 54
Starfruit and Pork
  Salad, 44
Stuffed Beancurd, 60
Stuffed Deep-fried
  Beancurd, 62
Sundanese Vegetable
  Salad, 34
Tauhu Goreng, 63
Taupok Pau, 62
Thai Beef Salad, 59
Thai Cucumber Salad, 10
Thai Cuttlefish Salad, 8
Thai Glass Noodles
  Salad, 52

Thai Green Mango
  Salad, 36
Thai Mackerel Salad, 27
Thai Mushroom Salad, 32
Thai Papaya Salad, 33
Thai Raw Fish Salad, 9
Urap, 21
Vietnamese Beansprout
  Salad, 29
Vietnamese Chicken
  Salad, 56
Vietnamese Cucumber
  Salad, 30
Vietnamese Papaya
  Salad, 28

Warm Salads
  Cabbage, Wood Ears and
    Chicken Kerabu, 38
  Chicken Kerabu, 40
  Grilled Aubergine, 35
  Karedog, 34
  Kerabu Chicken, 30
  Sambal Belacan, 5
  Sambal Timun, 42
  Shrimp Paste Chilli
    Dip, 15
  Spicy Peanut Dip, 5
  Spicy Scallops Salad, 24
  Starfruit and Pork
    Salad, 44
  Thai Green Mango
    Salad, 36
  Thai Mackerel Salad, 27
  Thai Mushroom
    Salad, 32
  Thai Papaya Salad, 33
  Thai Raw Vegetable Salad
    with Shrimp Paste
    Chilli Dip, 14
  Vietnamese Beansprout
    Salad, 29
  Vietnamese Cucumber
    Salad, 30
  Vietnamese Papaya
    Salad, 28
  Yu Sheng, 10